Get Rich Selling

Lucie Dupont

Lucie Dupont

Lucie Dupont

Copyright Page

Index

Lucie Dupont

Lucie Dupont

The Power of Sales

The power of sales is a transformative force that can change a person's life. Sales is not only the foundation of commerce, but an essential skill that anyone can learn to improve their financial and personal life. It is often thought that only a select few are "born" with the talent to sell, but the truth is that anyone can develop this skill with dedication and practice. Selling is not just about offering a product or service, but about understanding how to influence the decisions of others, how to communicate the value of what you have, and above all, how to help people solve their problems.

When we talk about sales, we are referring to a powerful tool that will not only allow you to earn more money, but will also help you grow as a person. By learning to sell, you are not only mastering a set of techniques to exchange goods or services for money, you are developing a skill that will stay with you throughout your life. Knowing how to sell opens doors that would otherwise remain closed. It allows you to connect with people, create valuable relationships, and generate opportunities anywhere and at any time. Selling is the ability to create solutions where others see problems, to find opportunities where others see obstacles.

Sales are everywhere. From the small shopkeeper offering his wares at the market to the multi-millionaire businessman closing gigantic contracts, everyone, in one way or another, is selling something. Even when you are not engaged in sales directly, you are always selling something, be it an idea, a proposal or even yourself. Think about a job interview: you are selling your experience and skills to the employer. On a date, you are selling your personality, your way of being. In a conversation with friends, you are selling your opinions. Sales is, in essence, a fundamental part of daily life.

Through sales, you can achieve a financial freedom that few traditional jobs offer. Unlike many jobs where your income is limited to a fixed salary, in sales your earnings depend on your results. If you get good at it, there is no limit to how much you can earn. Sales gives you the chance to generate your own income, to not depend on a boss or a company to know how much money you will receive at the end of the month. This, of course, requires effort and dedication. But once you master the art of selling, the rewards can be amazing. You can create your own business, be your own boss, and control your own destiny.

Selling is not just about exchanging a product for money. It is about creating value. The best salesperson is not the one who simply persuades someone to buy something they don't need. He is the one who identifies a need or a problem in his client and offers a real solution. When you achieve this, you create a relationship of trust, and when there is trust, sales flow naturally. People come back again and again because they know you can help them, that you can offer them something that really improves their lives or solves a problem they have. This is the real magic of sales: helping others while helping yourself.

Furthermore, sales teaches you skills that are useful in all areas of life. Through selling, you learn to communicate better, to negotiate, to persuade, to listen actively, to understand what the other person really needs. These are skills that will not only make you a better salesperson, but also a more well-rounded person. Communication is key in any relationship, whether personal or professional, and sales forces you to hone this skill.

Sales also teaches you to be resilient. In the world of sales, rejection is common, and many see it as an insurmountable obstacle. But this is where one of the great secrets of successful salespeople lies: they don't fear rejection, they see it as part of the process. They know that every "no" brings them closer to a "yes." Learning to handle rejection and not give up at the first difficulties is an invaluable life lesson that sales can teach you. Persistence is key in any area of success, and in sales it becomes an essential quality.

The beauty of sales is that you don't need a college degree to succeed. You don't need a huge initial investment. What you need is dedication, a willingness to learn, and the desire to constantly improve. Everyone can start selling at some level, whether it's your own product, a service, or even as a middleman selling other people's products. The key is to get started, learn from each experience, and never stop perfecting your technique.

The power of sales is the gateway to financial independence. It is the means to stop depending on a fixed salary and start building your own future. But beyond the financial rewards, sales also give you the opportunity to help others, improve their lives, and create meaningful relationships. No matter what stage of life you are in, you can always learn to sell, and by doing so, you will be taking an important step towards a more prosperous and fulfilling future.

In short, sales is an incredibly powerful tool. It's not just about money, it's about the ability to influence, to connect with others, to solve problems, and to create value. Through sales, you can not only become rich, but you can also transform your life on multiple levels. Selling is more than a profession, it's a way of life that, once you master it, will open up a world of limitless opportunities for you.

Lucie Dupont

How Great Salespeople Think

The mindset of great salespeople is what really sets them apart from everyone else. For them, selling isn't just an activity or a job; it's a way of looking at the world. While many people see the sales process as a difficult, stressful, or even unpleasant task, great salespeople see it as an opportunity. They know that every interaction with a customer is an open door to success, a chance to improve their skills, grow, and of course, increase their income. But it all starts with the way they think, the mindset they have when approaching each sale.

One of the key aspects of how great salespeople think is their belief in the product or service they are selling. For them, it's not just about making a sale, but about offering something that will truly help the customer. They have a deep conviction that what they are selling can make a difference in the life of the person who buys it. This belief is what gives them confidence when they speak, because they know they are offering something valuable. And that confidence is contagious. When a salesperson is confident that their product is great, that confidence is passed on to the customer and makes it much easier to make a sale.

Great salespeople also understand that rejection is part of the process. Where many might be discouraged by a "no," they view each rejection as one more step toward a "yes." They don't take rejection personally. They know it's not a reflection on them as a person or their ability as a salesperson. They simply understand that not every customer will be interested in what they have to offer at that moment, and that's okay. Instead of giving up, they learn from each situation, adjust their approach, and move on. To them, each "no" is just an opportunity to improve and get closer to the next sale.

Another important aspect of their mindset is perseverance. Great salespeople don't give up easily. They know that many times, the difference between success and failure in sales is the ability to keep trying. No matter how many times things don't go their way, they keep moving forward. This persistence allows them to overcome obstacles that would stop other people. They know that success in sales isn't always immediate, but that those who keep going, even when things get tough, are the ones who ultimately achieve great results.

Great salespeople are also extremely curious. They are always looking for ways to improve and learn more about their industry, their products, and most of all, their customers. They know that the more they understand their customers, the easier it will be to meet their needs. So they ask questions, listen carefully, and observe. This curiosity allows them to identify problems that the customer may not even have known they had, and gives them the opportunity to offer solutions that truly make a difference. They don't just sell, they help. And by helping, they create lasting relationships that result in loyal customers.

The ability to set clear goals is another key characteristic of the great salespeople's mindset. They don't go through life aimlessly, waiting for things to happen. Instead, they set specific goals and work with determination to achieve them. These goals are not only related to the number of sales they want to achieve, but also to personal and professional growth. They know that in order to improve as salespeople, they must constantly challenge themselves. They set goals that force them to step out of their comfort zone, and that extra effort is what allows them to stand out.

Great salespeople also have an abundance mindset. They don't think the market is limited or that other people's success takes away opportunities from them. Instead, they see a world full of possibilities and believe there is always more to offer, more people to help, and more deals to close. This mindset allows them to stay positive, even in times of difficulty. They know there will always be more opportunities to come if they continue to work hard and stay focused. They don't waste time worrying about what they don't have, but instead focus on creating more of what they want.

Empathy is another quality that defines great salespeople. They don't just see their customers as a source of income, but as people with real needs and wants. They put themselves in the customer's shoes and try to understand what they're really concerned about. This empathy allows them to connect on a deeper level and build trusting relationships. By understanding the customer, they can tailor their message in a way that better resonates with what the customer is looking for. Instead of just selling a product, they become trusted advisors who are truly there to help.

Discipline is a key characteristic of a great salesperson's mindset. They know that success doesn't come overnight and that small daily actions are what lead to great achievements. That's why they are consistent in their efforts. They have clear routines, they make sales calls, they keep looking for new clients, they review their goals and adjust their strategies. They don't rely on motivation to act, but on discipline to stay focused, even when they don't feel like doing so. They know that the key to success is consistency and that every small step counts.

Finally, great salespeople have a positive attitude toward challenges. Where others see problems, they see opportunities. They know that obstacles are inevitable, but they also know that every challenge is an opportunity to learn and grow. This optimistic attitude allows them to continue forward with enthusiasm, even when things don't go their way. Instead of focusing on the difficulties, they concentrate on finding solutions and moving forward.

In short, the way great salespeople think is what allows them to excel. Their confidence in the value of what they offer, their perseverance in the face of rejection, their curiosity to learn, their empathy toward customers, and their positive attitude toward challenges are the keys that lead them to success. They don't see sales as a simple exchange of products, but rather as an opportunity to improve the lives of others while achieving their own goals. By adopting this mindset, anyone can begin to think and act like a great salesperson and eventually reap the same results.

The Key to Selling More

The key to selling more is not being the most eloquent or having the best product, but rather knowing your customer deeply. This is the true essence of successful sales. If you don't know who you're selling to, you'll hardly be able to offer them something they really want or need. Many salespeople make the mistake of focusing only on their product or the features of what they're offering, but great salespeople know that the customer comes first. They understand that if they can identify what their customer is really looking for, what they're worried about, or what they need solved, selling will be a natural consequence.

Knowing your customer means much more than knowing their name or age. It means understanding what motivates them, what their problems are, their desires and aspirations. To sell more, you need to become a detective. This doesn't mean you have to ask intrusive questions or make the person uncomfortable, but you do have to be willing to listen more than you talk. Salespeople often think they have to be the ones leading the entire conversation, talking non-stop about the benefits of their product or service. However, the real magic of sales is in active listening. When you listen, you gain valuable clues about what your customer really needs.

Great salespeople are experts at asking the right questions. They don't settle for superficial answers, but instead dig deeper into the conversation to uncover their customer's deeper needs. They ask things like, "What are you most concerned about right now?" or "What solution would be ideal for you?" These questions open the door to meaningful conversations, and in those conversations, customers reveal key information that can be the difference between a successful sale or a customer who walks away without buying.

Another important aspect of knowing your customer is understanding their emotions. People don't just buy for logical reasons, they buy for emotional reasons too. In fact, most purchasing decisions are driven by emotions, even though we often don't realize it. People buy to feel better, to solve a problem that causes them anxiety, or to achieve a goal that gives them satisfaction. If you can identify which emotions are at play during the buying process, you'll be one step closer to making the sale. For example, if a customer is looking for insurance, they may actually be looking for peace of mind for their family. In that case, you're not just selling them insurance, you're selling them peace of mind.

To sell more, it's also crucial that you segment your customers. Not all customers are the same, and what works for one may not work for another. A common mistake is to treat all customers the same, when in reality, each has different needs and motivations. Some may be more concerned about price, while others value quality or service more. By understanding the differences between your customers, you can personalize your approach and offer them exactly what they need. This level of personalization will not only help you sell more, but it will also make customers feel valued and understood.

Another key point is that by knowing your customer, you also learn to identify the right moments to offer your product. In sales, timing is everything. Sometimes, you can have the right product and the right customer, but if it's not the right time for that person, the sale won't happen. That's why great salespeople know how to read the signals and recognize when is the best time to present their offer. This may mean waiting a little longer, or sometimes being more direct if they see that the customer is ready to make a decision.

Additionally, knowing your customer means understanding their environment and the factors that may influence their purchasing decision. For example, a customer may be interested in your product, but if their environment is not supportive or they are being influenced by other factors, they may hesitate to make the purchase. Great salespeople don't just sell to the individual, they also take into account external influences. This may include the opinion of their family, friends, or even market trends. Knowing how to handle these external influences will allow you to overcome objections and close more sales.

Knowing your customer also helps you anticipate their objections. Every customer has questions or concerns before making a purchase, and if you can anticipate them, you'll be better prepared to address them effectively. By listening and observing your customers, you can identify what they're concerned about. Is it the price? Is it the product's functionality? Is it the company's reputation? Once you identify these objections, you can resolve them before they become a problem. Great salespeople don't wait for the customer to voice their concerns; they proactively address them.

Finally, getting to know your customer isn't a one-time thing. It's an ongoing process. Customers change, their needs change, and you have to be willing to adapt. To sell more, you need to be constantly learning—not just about your products or services, but also about the people you're selling them to. This requires always being attentive to their needs, listening to their feedback, and adjusting your approach when necessary. Great salespeople know that the market is constantly evolving, and because of that, they're always looking for new ways to connect with their customers.

In short, the key to selling more is not being the best speaker or having the most impressive product. The real key is knowing your customer deeply, understanding their needs, their wants, and their concerns. By doing so, you can offer solutions that really matter and create relationships that last. Not only will this help you sell more, but it will also allow you to build a solid base of loyal customers who will come back to you again and again. Selling, at the end of the day, is an act of service. And the better you know those you serve, the more successful you will be.

Lucie Dupont

Create Irresistible Proposals

Creating irresistible propositions is one of the most powerful keys to selling more and closing deals consistently. It's not just about offering something good, but about presenting an offer that is so attractive to the customer that it's hard for them to say no. To achieve this, you must understand that an irresistible proposition does not depend solely on the price or the features of your product or service, but on how you make the customer see the value they can get. Often, customers don't buy just because of what they see, but because of how they feel about it. Your job is to make them feel excited, convinced and confident that your offer is the best option.

The first step to creating an irresistible proposition is to get to know your customer deeply. If you don't understand what your customer really needs or cares about, it will be difficult to craft an offer that speaks directly to them. For example, if you're selling a high-tech product to someone who isn't very tech-savvy, talking about technical features won't be effective. Instead, you should focus on how that product will make their life easier or solve a problem they have. For a proposition to be irresistible, it must address a specific and relevant customer need. This can only be achieved if you've done the work of listening and understanding first.

Once you're clear on what your customer needs, you need to focus on communicating the value of your offering in a way that's clear and compelling. This is where many salespeople go wrong: Instead of talking about how their product or service will benefit the customer, they focus on superficial features or comparisons to competitors. People don't buy products or services, they buy solutions to their problems. Your pitch should be focused on solving a problem or improving the customer's life in some meaningful way. The clearer and more direct you are in explaining how your offering will accomplish that, the more irresistible it will be.

Another crucial aspect of creating irresistible offers is adding something extra that makes the customer feel like they are getting exceptional value. This doesn't necessarily mean you should cut the price or give huge discounts. In fact, an irresistible offer isn't about being the cheapest option, but about offering something that makes the customer feel like they are getting much more than they expected. This "extra" can be something as simple as an additional service, a special bonus, a longer trial period, or an extended warranty. The important thing is that it is something that the customer perceives as valuable and that they can't easily find elsewhere.

Scarcity and urgency are also powerful elements in making a proposition irresistible. When people feel like they have unlimited time to make a decision, they tend to procrastinate or reconsider. However, if you make your offer limited in time or quantity, you're incentivizing the customer to act immediately. For example, you could offer a discount or bonus for a limited period only, or make the offer available only to the first people who accept it. The idea isn't to pressure the customer in an uncomfortable way, but to create a genuine sense of urgency that motivates them to take action before they miss the opportunity.

Trust is also a decisive factor in making a proposition irresistible. If the customer doesn't trust you or your product, it will be very difficult for them to accept any offer, no matter how attractive it may seem. This is where guarantees play an important role. Offering a solid guarantee that eliminates the risk for the customer can make them feel much more secure in making a decision. A money-back guarantee, for example, sends the message that you are so confident in your product or service that you are willing to give the money back if it does not meet the customer's expectations. This reduces the feeling of risk and increases the likelihood that the customer will say yes.

A common mistake many salespeople make when creating proposals is overloading the customer with too much information. When an offer is too complicated or confusing, the customer feels overwhelmed and is more likely to postpone the purchase decision. An irresistible proposal should be simple, clear, and easy to understand. If you can explain the benefits of your offer in a few words, you'll be on the right track. Simplicity is key because it reduces mental barriers customers may have. If your proposal is direct and to the point, the customer won't have to work hard to understand why they should accept it.

Another important component of an irresistible proposition is showing that others have already seen positive results with what you offer. People trust the experience of others, and social proof, such as testimonials, case studies, or recommendations, can make all the difference. When a customer sees that others have had success with your product or service, they feel more secure and confident that it will be a good decision for them, too. If you can include genuine testimonials from customers who have seen results thanks to your offer, your proposition becomes much more compelling.

On top of all this, an irresistible offer must be personalized. Not all customers are the same, and a generic offer will rarely have the same impact as one tailored to the customer's specific needs. If you can show that your offer has been created with that person or company's particularities in mind, the customer will feel like they are receiving something special. Personalizing the offer doesn't mean you have to make a radical change in what you offer, but you do have to present the information in a way that the customer feels it perfectly fits what he or she needs.

Finally, the presentation of your proposal is also critical. It doesn't matter how good your offer is if the way you present it doesn't capture the client's attention. An attractive, clear, and well-organized presentation can make an average offer seem much more valuable. Pay attention to the details of how you deliver your proposal, whether in person, in writing, or digitally. Make sure it's visually appealing and that the client can immediately identify the benefits they will gain by accepting your offer.

In short, creating irresistible proposals is not just about lowering prices or making aggressive offers. It is about deeply understanding your customer, communicating the value of what you offer clearly and directly, and adding elements that make the offer perceived as unique and valuable. Simplicity, urgency, trust, and personalization are the pillars on which the best proposals are built. When you manage to combine these elements effectively, you will not only increase your sales, but you will also create long-lasting relationships with customers who will be happy to have accepted your offer.

Master the Sales Process

Mastering the sales process is critical for anyone who wants to succeed in the world of sales. While every sale is unique and every customer has their own needs, the sales process follows certain universal steps that, if you understand and master them well, will allow you to increase your chances of closing deals consistently. The sales process is like a guide, a series of stages that help you take a potential customer from initial interest to final purchase. The better you master each of these stages, the smoother the process will be and, therefore, the more sales you will achieve.

The first step in the sales process is prospecting, which involves identifying potential customers. This is one of the most important aspects because without prospects, there are simply no sales. Many salespeople make the mistake of trying to sell to everyone, but the reality is that not everyone is an ideal customer for what you are offering. You need to be able to identify those who actually have the potential to benefit from your product or service. This is where research and analysis skills come into play. Who is your target audience? What kind of people or companies need what you are selling? Good prospecting saves you time and effort, because it allows you to focus on those who are most likely to become customers.

Once you have identified your prospects, the next step is the initial contact. This is the moment when you introduce yourself to the client and get their attention. It can be through a phone call, an email, an in-person meeting, or even through social media. The important thing here is that the first contact is engaging enough to generate interest. You have to be clear, concise, and direct. Don't try to sell right away. The goal of this first contact is to start a conversation and build a relationship. Think of this step as an opportunity to open the door to a trusting relationship with the client.

After the initial contact, it's time to do some more in-depth research into the customer's needs. This stage is known as qualification. Not every prospect you contact will be a good lead, so you need to ask key questions to determine if they really need what you offer, if they can afford it, and if they have the authority to make a purchasing decision. This is the time to find out what their problems are, what solutions they're looking for, and what expectations they have. Open-ended questions are very useful at this stage because they allow the customer to talk more and give you more information. Remember, your job here is not just to sell, but to understand how you can help solve their problems.

Once you have qualified the prospect and know that they are a suitable potential customer, the presentation stage comes. This is the phase where you present your product or service and explain how it can benefit the customer. This is where many salespeople get excited and talk non-stop about the features of what they are offering, but that is a mistake. The most important thing in this phase is not what you think is great about your product, but how your product or service can solve the customer's specific problems. The presentation should be focused on them, not you. That is why it is crucial that you tailor your message to what you have already learned about the customer during the qualification phase. Make your presentation personalized, clear, and focused on the most relevant benefits.

The next step in the sales process is handling objections. It's normal for customers to have doubts, questions, or concerns before making a decision. They might be worried about the price, unsure if your product is what they really need, or uncertain about how it will work in their particular situation. Instead of seeing objections as an obstacle, you should see them as an opportunity to provide more information and clear up any misunderstandings. If you've done your job well up to this point, handling objections will be much easier, because you'll already have a good idea of what the customer is concerned about. The key here is to listen carefully and respond calmly and reasonably, showing that you understand their concerns and have the solution.

After handling objections, it's time to close the sale. This is one of the most crucial moments of the process and also one of the most feared by many salespeople. Closing is simply asking the customer to make a decision. Although some salespeople see it as awkward or aggressive, in reality, if you've followed the process well up to this point, closing should feel like a natural continuation of the conversation. There are many closing techniques, from asking direct questions like "Would you like to proceed with this option?" to more subtle techniques like summarizing the benefits and asking which one they would like to start using. The important thing is that you do it in a confident and calm manner, without fear of receiving a "no." Remember, closing is not the end, but the beginning of a long-term relationship of trust with the customer.

However, the sales process doesn't end with the close. Once the customer has made the decision to buy, the follow-up phase is vital. This step is often overlooked by many salespeople, but it's one of the most important. After the sale, you need to make sure the customer is happy with their purchase and that any issues or concerns they have are resolved promptly. Good follow-up not only ensures customer satisfaction, but it also opens the door to future sales opportunities, whether through upselling or referrals. Happy customers are more likely to recommend you to others, meaning good follow-up can lead to even more sales in the future.

Finally, throughout the entire sales process, it's important to maintain a positive attitude and a customer-oriented approach. Sales aren't just a transaction; they're an opportunity to help someone improve their life or business. If you approach each stage of the process with a mindset of service and providing real value, you'll not only be more successful at closing sales, but you'll also build stronger, longer-lasting relationships with your customers.

In short, mastering the sales process requires understanding each of its stages and knowing how to execute them effectively. From prospecting to follow-up, each step is important and plays a key role in overall success. It's not just about following a script, but about adapting to each situation and each client, listening and responding to their needs. When you master this process, you not only close more sales, but you also become a more well-rounded professional and someone clients can trust.

Understanding Your Mind to Sell More

Understanding the minds of your customers is one of the most valuable skills you can develop as a salesperson. If you can understand how they think, what their motivations are, and what drives them to make decisions, you'll be one step ahead in being able to positively influence them and make the sales process much easier. Often, when a salesperson fails to meet their goals, it's not because they have a bad product or aren't working hard enough, but because they're failing to connect with what the customer really wants or needs. Selling more isn't always about talking more, but about knowing how to listen and read between the lines. It's about getting into the customer's mind and understanding what drives them to act.

One of the first things you need to understand about the customer's mind is that most purchasing decisions are not entirely rational, but emotional. Although people often say they make logical decisions, in reality, much of what they buy is driven by emotions. Whether it's the desire to feel secure, the need for recognition, or the search for personal satisfaction, emotions play a key role in any purchasing decision. That's why it's important that, as a seller, you don't just focus on the technical or functional features of what you offer, but on how it makes the customer feel. Ask yourself: What emotional problem is my product solving? How can I make the customer feel better, happier, or more confident with this purchase?

Another important thing to keep in mind is that people often buy for their own reasons, not because you are selling them. In other words, the customer is always thinking about their own interests, not yours. This means that in order to sell more, you need to be able to align what you offer with the customer's wants and needs. Sometimes, as salespeople, we get carried away by the excitement of what we are selling and forget that, at the end of the day, the customer is thinking, "What's in it for me?" That's why it's critical to put yourself in the customer's shoes and see things from their perspective. When you do, you can tailor your approach and message to resonate with what really matters to them.

A crucial aspect of understanding the customer's mind is knowing that people often have fears and insecurities that can hold them back from making a purchase decision. Even if a customer is interested in your product, they may have doubts or concerns about whether it's really the best option, whether it's worth the money, or whether it will meet their expectations. This is where your ability to reduce those insecurities and make the customer feel more confident comes into play. Offering guarantees, sharing testimonials from other satisfied customers, or simply listening to their concerns and answering them clearly and honestly can help dispel those fears. Remember, a customer with doubts doesn't buy, but if you manage to give them the peace of mind they need, you'll be much closer to closing the sale.

Customer behavior is also greatly influenced by what others do or think. This phenomenon, known as "social proof," is one of the most powerful tools in the world of sales. People tend to feel more comfortable making a decision when they see that others have done the same thing with good results. That's why reviews, testimonials, and success stories are so effective. If a customer sees that others have purchased and are happy with what you offer, they are more likely to be inclined to follow that same path. Understanding this principle allows you to use social proof to your advantage, showing how your product or service has made a difference in the lives of others.

A common mistake many salespeople make is assuming that all customers think the same way. This is far from the truth. Every customer is unique, with their own experiences, values, and priorities. Some are motivated by price, others by quality, and others by convenience. Therefore, part of understanding your customer's mind involves being able to identify what their top priority is. Some will be more concerned with getting the best deal, while others will want to make sure they are receiving the most unique product. You need to adjust your approach based on what is most important to the customer you are dealing with at the time. Actively listening and asking questions is key to finding out what each particular customer really cares about.

Another important thing to know is that people often need to feel like they are making the decision for themselves, even if you are the one guiding them through that process. People don't want to feel manipulated or pressured. Instead of trying to force a sale, it's better to take a guiding approach, where you help the customer come to their own conclusion. Ask questions that lead them to reflect on their needs and how your product can meet them. When customers feel like they have freely made a decision, they are more likely to be satisfied with their purchase and not regret it later. This also helps you build a relationship of trust, as the customer will feel like you are interested in helping them rather than just selling them something.

The customer's mind is also deeply influenced by the sense of urgency and scarcity. If people feel like they have all the time in the world to make a decision, they are likely to put off the purchase. However, when they perceive that they have a limited opportunity, either due to time or availability, they are more inclined to act immediately. That's why many sales strategies include limited-time offers or exclusive promotions. When you genuinely introduce a sense of urgency, the customer feels the need to make a decision before they lose the opportunity. But be careful not to overuse this tactic. If the customer perceives the urgency as false or forced, you may lose their trust.

In addition to all of the above, understanding the mind of the customer also means being aware that sometimes purchasing decisions are driven by the desire to avoid pain rather than seeking pleasure. For example, a person may be more motivated to buy health insurance to avoid the risk of huge medical expenses than by the pleasure of having protection. In sales, this means that instead of just focusing on the positive benefits of what you offer, you can also address what the customer might lose if they don't take action. Showing the potential consequences of not taking action can be a powerful motivator, as long as you do so honestly and without exaggeration.

Finally, one of the keys to understanding the customer's mind is knowing that trust is the deciding factor in many purchases. A customer will only buy if they trust you, your product, and your company. That trust is built over time, through every interaction you have with the customer. From the first contact to the follow-up after the sale, everything you do and say has an impact on how the customer perceives you. Being honest, keeping your promises, and showing a genuine interest in helping your customers are all ways to strengthen that trust. Remember, sales are not just about transactions, they are about relationships.

In short, understanding the customer's mind is the foundation for selling more. Buying decisions are driven by emotions, fears, needs and desires. If you can read between the lines and connect with what really motivates your customers, you'll have a huge advantage over those salespeople who only focus on talking about their product. Listen, adapt your approach, build trust and make the customer feel like they're making the best decision for them. When you master this art, you'll not only close more sales, but you'll also create long-lasting relationships and satisfied customers who will come back to buy from you again and again.

The Art of Negotiation

Negotiation is one of the most important skills for any salesperson to master. Although many think that selling and negotiating are the same thing, they are actually two different things. Selling is about offering something that the customer needs or wants, while negotiation is the process by which agreements are reached that benefit both the seller and the customer. Negotiating is an art, because there is no single formula that works in every situation. Every negotiation is unique, as every customer is different, with their own needs, expectations, and concerns. If you can learn to negotiate well, you will have a significant advantage, not only because you will close more deals, but because you will achieve agreements that satisfy both parties.

The first step to mastering the art of negotiation is to prepare properly. Many salespeople make the mistake of thinking that negotiation starts when they are in front of the customer, but in reality it starts much earlier. Preparing means knowing your product or service well, understanding the strengths you can highlight, and being aware of potential objections or concerns the customer may have. It's also important to know the customer. What are they most interested in? What do they value most: price, quality, speed of delivery? The more you know about the customer and their needs before you sit down to negotiate, the better prepared you'll be to reach an agreement that works for both of you.

One of the keys to successful negotiation is understanding that it's not always about winning or losing. The best negotiations are those where both parties feel like they've gained something. This is called a "win-win" deal. A common misconception is that for you to win, the customer has to lose, or vice versa. But the reality is that when both parties are happy with the deal, that business relationship is more likely to thrive in the long run. This means that when you negotiate, you shouldn't just focus on getting what you want, but also on making sure the customer gets something valuable. The key is to find a middle ground where both parties feel benefited.

Active listening is a powerful tool in any negotiation. Many salespeople go into a negotiation thinking that their job is to talk and convince the customer to agree to their terms. But in reality, one of the most important aspects of negotiation is being a good listener. Listening carefully to what the customer has to say will allow you to better understand what their concerns are, what they really want, and what they are willing to negotiate for. Sometimes customers don't directly express what they are looking for, but if you pay attention to their words and nonverbal language, you can identify key clues that will help you adjust your strategy.

Another key aspect of negotiation is flexibility. You won't always get exactly what you want, and that's okay. Negotiating doesn't mean being rigid or sticking to one point of view. In fact, one of the biggest mistakes you can make is being inflexible. If you go into a negotiation with a closed mindset, the customer is likely to feel like there's no room for dialogue, which can cause you to lose the sale entirely. Being flexible doesn't mean giving in on everything, but rather being willing to explore different options. Maybe you can't lower the price, but you can offer a more convenient payment plan. Or maybe you can't make delivery faster, but you can add extra value that makes the offer more attractive to the customer. The idea is to be willing to negotiate on certain aspects in order to reach an agreement that works for both parties.

It's also important to be clear about your limits before you enter into a negotiation. This refers to what you're willing to give up and what you're not. If you're not clear about this, it's easy to get carried away by the pressure of the moment and end up accepting a deal that doesn't benefit you. Before you negotiate, ask yourself: What's the best outcome I can get? What's the minimum I'm willing to accept? Knowing how far you can go gives you an advantage, because it allows you to stand firm on certain key points without losing control of the negotiation. At the same time, it also gives you the freedom to give in in other areas without feeling like you're sacrificing too much.

A good negotiator also knows how to manage time. Negotiation is not something that should be rushed. Sometimes the best strategy is to take time to think or give the client space to reflect. If you feel like the negotiation is stuck, don't be afraid to take a break. Taking a break can help both parties reconsider their positions and come back with a more open perspective. Plus, giving the client time to think shows that you're not desperate to close the deal, which can make them feel less pressured, too. Remember that patience is a virtue in negotiation. Quick deals aren't always the best.

Another important technique is to use the power of silence. Often, salespeople feel the need to fill every moment of the negotiation with words, but silence can be a very powerful tool. When you make an offer or propose a change, you don't always have to keep talking. Sometimes, it's better to keep quiet and let the customer think. Silence can create a little tension that motivates the customer to make a decision or make a counteroffer. Plus, it gives you time to observe the customer's reactions and adjust your approach as needed.

It's also important not to take negotiations personally. Sometimes clients can be harsh or even seem unreasonable, but you need to remember that this is part of the process. If you take every objection or comment personally, you're likely to get frustrated or lose your cool. Negotiations should be professional at all times. If the client is being difficult, instead of responding negatively, try to understand where their concerns are coming from. Stay calm and continue to look for a solution that works for both of you. Strong emotions can cloud your judgment and cause you to make poor decisions. A good negotiator knows how to keep their cool, even in tense situations.

Finally, it is essential to close the negotiation in a clear and firm manner. Once both parties have reached an agreement, it is important to make sure that all the terms are understood and accepted by both parties. Sometimes, after a long negotiation, people can assume things or take certain details for granted, which can cause problems later on. Make sure that everything is clear, either with a firm verbal agreement or in writing, if necessary. This not only prevents misunderstandings, but also shows that you are a professional who takes care of every detail of the process.

In short, the art of negotiation is a combination of preparation, active listening, flexibility, and patience. It's not about asserting yourself or winning at any cost, but about finding solutions that benefit both parties. Being a good negotiator takes practice, but once you master these skills, you'll find that you'll not only close more sales, but also build stronger, longer-lasting relationships with your clients. Negotiating well is not just a useful skill in sales, but in life in general. When you understand how to handle the process effectively, you can achieve more than you ever imagined, both in business and in every aspect of your daily life.

Lucie Dupont

Building Long-Term Relationships

Building long-term relationships with your customers is one of the most important keys to success in sales. Many salespeople focus only on closing a quick sale and forget about the most important thing: maintaining a long-term relationship with the customer. If you think of the sale as a one-time transaction, you're missing out on great opportunities. The most successful sales don't happen just once, but are built on a foundation of trust and loyalty that is cultivated over time. When you manage to create long-term relationships with your customers, they not only come back to buy from you again and again, but they also recommend you to others. In other words, building long-term relationships is an investment in your future success.

The first thing you need to understand about long-term relationships is that they are built on trust. If a customer trusts you, they are much more likely to come back, even if there are other options on the market. But trust isn't earned overnight. It's something you build through every interaction with the customer. From the first conversation to the follow-up after the sale, every step you take is an opportunity to show the customer that you are trustworthy, that you keep your promises, and that you really care about helping them. If you do this consistently, the customer will start to see you not just as a salesperson, but as an ally, someone they can rely on for the long term.

An important factor in building long-term relationships is being authentic. Customers can easily tell when a salesperson isn't being sincere or when they're just trying to close a sale quickly. If you want your relationships with customers to last, you have to be genuine in your interest in them and their needs. This means that you shouldn't just focus on selling what you want, but on finding the best solution for the customer, even if that means recommending something that won't bring you immediate profit. When the customer feels that you truly care about their well-being and not just your own benefit, they will begin to trust you more, which lays the foundation for a long-term relationship.

Communication is another fundamental pillar for building long-term relationships. Keeping in touch with your customers on a regular basis, without being invasive, is key to keeping the relationship alive. It's not about calling or texting all the time just to sell them something, but rather maintaining useful and relevant communication. Maybe you could send them information on how to get more out of a product they already bought or remind them that they have a special discount for being a frequent customer. Small gestures like these make the customer feel valued and show that you don't see them as just another number, but as an important person for your business.

Following up after a sale is crucial. Many salespeople forget about the customer once the deal has been closed, but this is precisely the time when the relationship can either strengthen or weaken. After a sale, it is important to make sure the customer is happy with their purchase and that they do not have any questions or issues. A simple follow-up message asking if everything is okay or if you need to offer any additional assistance can make a huge difference. Not only does this show that you care about their satisfaction, but it also opens the door for future interactions and sales.

Another way to build long-term relationships is by offering excellent customer service. No matter how good your product is, if a customer has a bad experience with you, they are unlikely to return. Customer service is not limited to solving problems when they arise, but rather always being available and willing to help. Sometimes a customer may have questions about something that seems obvious, but it is important to respond with patience and kindness. How you treat your customers in those times of need is what can really set you apart from the competition. If customers know they can always count on you, not just to sell them something, but to provide support when they need it, they are much more likely to see you as someone they want to do business with long-term.

Empathy also plays a crucial role in building long-lasting relationships. Putting yourself in the customer's shoes and understanding their concerns, fears, and desires allows you to connect with them on a deeper level. Selling is not just about products or services, but about people. Every customer has a story, a particular situation, and when you show empathy, you create a bond that goes beyond the transaction. By taking the time to understand what the customer is really looking for, you can offer solutions that better fit their needs, which strengthens the relationship and increases the likelihood that they will come back to you in the future.

Another key to maintaining long-term relationships is to always be willing to learn and improve. The market changes, customer needs evolve, and you must be willing to adapt as well. This doesn't just mean improving your knowledge about the products you offer, but also paying attention to your customers' opinions and feedback. If a customer gives you constructive criticism or suggests an improvement, take it seriously. Listening to what your customers have to say and adjusting your approach when necessary is an effective way to show them that you value their opinion and are committed to offering the best service possible.

Customer loyalty can also be cultivated through reciprocity. When a customer feels like they've received something of value, they're more likely to be loyal to you. This doesn't always have to be a discount or a promotion, although those things help. It can also be something as simple as offering helpful information, giving sincere advice, or going the extra mile to resolve a problem. The key is to make sure the customer always feels like they're getting more than they expected. When you manage to exceed your customers' expectations, they see you as someone they can rely on for the long term.

Finally, don't underestimate the power of gratitude. A simple "thank you" can go a long way for a relationship. Thanking your customers for their business, their time, and their trust is an effective way to strengthen the relationship. Gratitude shows that you don't take their support for granted and that you value the relationship. This can be as simple as sending a thank you note after a purchase or simply thanking them during a conversation. These small gestures can leave a lasting impression and make the customer feel valued.

In short, building long-term relationships with your customers is a strategy that will bring you many more benefits than just looking for a quick sale. It's about cultivating trust, being authentic, maintaining constant communication, and offering excellent customer service. Empathy, willingness to improve, and gratitude are essential elements to create relationships that last over time. When you manage to establish these types of relationships, you not only ensure recurring sales, but you also become the first option in the customer's mind every time they need what you offer. Long-term relationships are the key to sustainable success in sales, and the sooner you start focusing on them, the sooner you will see the fruits.

Multiply Your Income with Cross-Selling and Upselling

Multiplying your revenue with cross-selling and upselling is a highly effective strategy you can use to maximize the value of each customer and increase your profits. While at first glance it may seem like these techniques are meant to make you sell more, in reality, they are all about offering more value to your customers and improving their overall experience. Let's break down how each of these strategies works and how you can implement them to significantly boost your revenue.

First, let's talk about cross-selling. This technique involves offering additional products or services that complement what the customer is already buying. The idea is to present the customer with options that can enhance their initial purchase or that are useful to them in combination with the main product. For example, if a customer is buying a camera, you could also offer them an additional memory card, a protective case, or a tripod. The key is to make sure that these additional products actually complement the main purchase and provide real value to the customer. Cross-selling isn't about selling something just for the sake of it, but about suggesting items that help the customer get the most out of their purchase.

For cross-selling to be effective, you need to have a good understanding of what your customers might need in addition to their main purchase. This requires knowing the products or services you offer and how they work together. It's also helpful to pay attention to customer purchasing trends and behavioral patterns. If you notice that certain products are often purchased together, you can make those recommendations part of your sales strategy. For example, if you sell beauty products, you could offer a skincare set that includes cleansers, toners, and creams, so the customer has everything they need for a complete routine.

Upselling, on the other hand, is a technique that focuses on persuading the customer to purchase a more expensive or upgraded version of the product or service they were initially considering. The idea here is that rather than simply selling more products, you focus on increasing the value of the customer's purchase. For example, if a customer is interested in purchasing a basic laptop, you could offer them a version with additional features, such as more RAM or a faster processor, that will give them better performance. The goal is to show the customer why the more expensive option is worth it and how it can improve their experience or better meet their needs.

To upsell effectively, it's critical to understand the customer's needs and preferences. It's not about forcing a more expensive sale just for the sake of it, but about showing the customer the additional benefits they'll get from spending a little more. This requires good product knowledge and the ability to clearly communicate the added value. If you can convincingly explain how the more expensive option will provide a superior experience or solve additional problems, the customer will be more willing to consider the purchase.

Both techniques, cross-selling and upselling, work best when they are aligned with a genuine interest in improving the customer experience. If you only focus on increasing your profits without considering what the customer really needs, you might come across as too pushy or even insincere. Instead, think about how you can make the customer feel satisfied and well-served with the additional options you are offering them. Not only will this help you increase your revenue, but it will also improve the customer's perception of your company, as they will feel valued and well-cared for.

To implement these strategies effectively, it's helpful to follow a few best practices. First, make sure the additional options you offer are relevant and of high quality. There's no point in recommending products that the customer won't find useful or that don't live up to their expectations. Also, present the options in a clear and non-invasive manner. It's important for the customer to feel like they're making an informed decision, not being pressured into buying more. You can do this by offering detailed information and allowing the customer to take their time to decide.

Another key practice is to personalize your recommendations based on the customer's profile. Use the information you have about their previous purchases, preferences, and behavior to make more accurate suggestions. If you know your customer and understand their needs, you'll be able to offer recommendations that will really interest them and fit well with what they're already searching for. Not only will this increase the chances of them accepting your offers, but it will also strengthen the relationship you have with them, as you'll be showing that you really understand their needs.

An important aspect of upselling and cross-selling is the moment you choose to present them. Doing so at the right time is crucial to the success of the strategy. For example, if you are making an online sale, you can display complementary products on the checkout page or in the purchase process. If you are in a physical store, you can present upselling options when the customer is considering their purchase or at the moment when they have already shown interest in a specific product. The goal is to take advantage of the customer's interest in their current purchase to make recommendations that seem natural and useful in that context.

It's also important to measure and analyze the results of your cross-selling and upselling strategies. Observe how customers respond to your recommendations and what impact they have on your revenue. Analyze which types of products or services sell best together and adjust your approach based on the data you gain. This information will allow you to continually improve your strategies and adapt your offerings to maximize your results.

Additionally, training your sales team is crucial to the success of these strategies. Make sure that all members of your team understand how cross-selling and upselling work and know how to apply them effectively. Provide examples and practices so that they feel comfortable making recommendations and presenting additional options to customers. A well-trained team will be much more effective at implementing these strategies and generating higher revenue.

In short, cross-selling and upselling are powerful techniques that can help you multiply your revenue and improve the customer experience. It involves offering additional products or services that complement the main purchase or persuading the customer to consider a more advanced option. By doing so in a relevant, clear and personalized way, you can increase the value of each sale and strengthen your relationship with the customer. Don't forget to measure the results and train your team to ensure the success of these strategies. When you apply them correctly, you will see how your revenue increases and your customers feel more satisfied with the value they receive.

How to Manage and Grow Your Wealth

Managing and growing your wealth is one of the most important aspects if you want to be financially successful in the long run. Many people think that making money is the final step, but in reality, once you start generating income, the most important thing is to learn how to manage that money wisely. It's not just about how much money you can make, but how you manage and grow it over time. If you don't manage your wealth well, even a large amount of money can quickly disappear. In this chapter, I'll explain the key steps you need to take to manage and grow your wealth in a sustained and conscious way.

The first step to managing your wealth is to create a solid financial plan. This plan should include all of your income, expenses, debts, investments, and anything else related to your finances. Planning is crucial because it allows you to have a clear vision of where you are today and where you want to go. Without a plan, it's easy to get lost in the day-to-day details and spend money aimlessly. A good financial plan gives you direction and helps you stay focused on your goals. Start by writing down all of your income and all of your expenses, both big and small. This will give you a clear picture of how you're using your money and where you might be wasting resources.

Once you have a plan, the next step is to set up a budget. A budget is simply a way to organize your income and expenses so that you know exactly how much you can afford to spend in each area of your life. When you have a budget, you can control your finances more effectively and avoid spending more than you earn. The goal is to live within your means while still saving and investing a portion of your income. The key to a good budget is to be realistic. It's not about depriving yourself of everything you enjoy, but rather making sure your money is working for you and not the other way around. If you follow your budget with discipline, you'll see your wealth begin to grow steadily.

Saving is another critical component of wealth management. No matter how much you earn, you should always set aside a portion of your income for savings. This habit will allow you to build a financial cushion that will protect you in times of emergency and give you the freedom to take advantage of opportunities when they arise. Saving doesn't mean putting away whatever you have left over at the end of the month; it means deciding in advance how much you're going to save and treating it as a priority. A good starting point is to save at least 10% of your income. If you can save more, all the better. Saving gives you financial security and is one of the strongest foundations for growing your wealth.

After you've made sure you're saving consistently, the next step is investing. Putting money away in a savings account is fine, but if you really want to grow your wealth, you need to put that money to work through investments. Investing allows you to earn returns on your money, meaning you can earn more over time without having to work harder. There are many ways to invest, from the stock market to real estate, mutual funds, bonds, and even owning a business. The key is to educate yourself about the different options and choose the ones that best fit your financial goals and risk tolerance. Not all investments are right for everyone, and some involve more risk than others. However, the basic rule is that the sooner you start investing, the faster you can see your money grow.

Another important aspect of managing your wealth is minimizing your debt. Not all debt is bad, but it can often become a burden if not managed properly. If you have debt, especially high-interest debt like credit cards, it is crucial that you pay it off as soon as possible. Every dollar you pay in interest is money you could be using to save or invest. While some types of debt, like mortgages or education loans, may be necessary and manageable, you should avoid going into debt for unnecessary expenses or impulse purchases. Debt, if left unchecked, can drain your resources and hinder the growth of your wealth.

As you manage your wealth, it's also important to always be on the lookout for ways to increase your income. Managing what you already have is key, but finding new sources of income can speed up your path to wealth. This can include starting your own business, developing new skills that will allow you to get a better job, or finding investment opportunities that generate passive income. Passive income is one of the best ways to grow your wealth, as it's money that keeps coming in without you having to actively work for it. Examples of passive income include rental property, stock dividends, or royalties from a book or product you've created.

Once you start earning more income, it's critical that you don't fall into the trap of increasing your expenses at the same rate. Many people, when they start earning more money, also start spending more, and in the end, fail to accumulate wealth. To avoid this, it's important to keep your expenses under control and make sure that a portion of your additional income goes directly into savings or investments. Financial discipline is what will truly allow you to maintain and grow your wealth in the long term. Every time your income increases, make sure to review your financial plan and adjust your budget to align with your new goals.

Another key aspect of growing your wealth is diversification. Diversification means not putting all your money into one investment or source of income. By diversifying, you reduce the risk of losing everything if one investment doesn't turn out the way you hoped. You can diversify by investing in different types of assets, such as stocks, bonds, real estate, or even your own business. Diversification allows you to protect your wealth while still taking advantage of different growth opportunities. The more diversified you are, the more stable your financial situation will be in the long run, and the more opportunities you will have to grow your wealth.

Financial education is another critical component to managing and growing your wealth. If you don't understand how finances work, it's easy to make poor decisions that can cost you dearly. Investing in your financial education is one of the best investments you can make. This means reading books on finances, taking courses, attending seminars, and generally learning as much as you can about how to effectively manage your money. The more you know, the more confident you'll be in making smart financial decisions and the more prepared you'll be to take advantage of opportunities that come your way.

Finally, it's important to have a long-term mindset when it comes to managing and growing your wealth. Wealth isn't built overnight, and you're likely to face some ups and downs along the way. However, if you keep a long-term view and remain disciplined with your finances, you'll see your wealth grow over time. Don't get carried away by emotions or short-term trends; instead, stay focused on your goals and keep working steadily toward them. Patience and consistency are two of the most important qualities for achieving financial success.

In short, managing and growing your wealth requires a combination of planning, discipline, and education. Creating a financial plan, saving consistently, investing wisely, and minimizing your debt are the pillars of good wealth management. Additionally, always looking for new ways to generate income and diversifying your investments will help you accelerate your financial growth. Remember that the key to success is having a long-term mindset and staying focused on your goals, even when things get tough. If you follow these principles, you will be on the right path to building wealth that will last over time.

Reinvest Smartly to Scale Your Business

Reinvesting wisely is one of the most powerful secrets to growing a business sustainably. It's not just about making money and putting it in a bank account. If you really want to scale your business, you need to learn how to put that money to work again, so that every penny you earn becomes an engine that drives your company's growth. Reinvesting means taking a portion of profits and allocating them to strategic areas of your business that can generate more revenue in the future. This process is crucial if your goal is to expand, reach more customers, and ultimately make your business much more profitable.

The first step to reinvesting wisely is to have a clear vision of where your business is today and where you want to take it. If you are not clear about which areas need improvement or where you can find growth opportunities, you could end up spending money on things that do not generate a real return. So, before reinvesting, take the time to analyze your operations, study your customers and evaluate the market. Ask yourself which areas could have the most impact on the growth of your business if they were given more attention.

It could be improving your product or service, expanding into new markets, training your team or developing new marketing strategies. Knowing exactly where to invest is what will make the difference between growing effectively and simply spending money without results.

One of the most common and effective places to reinvest is in marketing. Well-executed advertising and marketing can take your business to the next level by attracting more customers and increasing your visibility. If your marketing has been limited or unstrategic up until now, reinvesting in this area can be a great opportunity. Today, digital platforms offer many ways to reach your target audience, from social media to search engine advertising to content marketing. The important thing here is to not just spend money on marketing, but to do so strategically. Clearly define who your ideal customers are and what channels they use to consume information. Then, create campaigns specifically designed to attract those customers. A good return on investment in marketing can mean a steady stream of new customers that will help increase your revenue significantly.

Another key area you can reinvest in is improving your product or service. While it's important to invest in attracting new customers, it's also important to make sure that what you offer actually meets their expectations, or even exceeds them. Sometimes, improving your product or service can be the most effective way to ensure that the customers you already have continue to buy from you and speak highly of your business. Customer loyalty is critical to growth, and quality products are one of the surest ways to build it. Consider investing in research and development to make improvements, add new features, or solve problems that your customers have pointed out. You can also use your customers' feedback to identify the most urgent areas for improvement and work on them. By making your product or service the best it can be, you'll be creating a solid foundation for growth.

The team you have is another crucial asset you should think about reinvesting in. A business is only as good as the people who run it, and if you have a well-trained and motivated team, your business will be much more likely to succeed. Consider allocating a portion of your profits to training and developing your staff. This may mean offering additional training, improving working conditions, or even hiring more people to ease the workload. If your employees are well-trained and satisfied, they will be more productive and more committed to the success of the business. Plus, a strong and competent team will allow you to delegate more tasks, giving you more time to focus on growth and expansion strategies.

Reinvesting in technology can also be a great way to scale your business. Today, technology plays a key role in operational efficiency and the ability to reach new markets. Depending on the nature of your business, you might consider investing in software that helps you better manage your operations, automate certain processes, or improve the customer experience. For example, if you run an online store, investing in a more advanced e-commerce platform or data analytics tools can help you optimize your sales and get to know your customers better. If you run a service business, investing in technology that improves your team's productivity or makes it easier to communicate with customers can make a big difference in your ability to grow.

Additionally, it's important to consider geographic expansion as a potential area for reinvestment. If your business has achieved some success in a local market, reinvesting in opening new locations or expanding to other cities or countries can be a great way to scale. Of course, this requires careful planning and thorough research into the new market you're targeting. However, if you find the right market and approach it strategically, expansion can significantly increase your revenue and brand visibility. This type of reinvestment typically involves higher risk, but the rewards can also be much greater if done correctly.

Another smart reinvestment strategy is to strengthen your relationship with your current customers. While it's always exciting to attract new customers, you shouldn't forget that existing customers are one of your biggest sources of revenue. They already know your business, and if they're satisfied, they're likely to buy again. Reinvesting in customer loyalty can include rewards programs, improved customer service, or even creating personalized experiences that make your customers feel valued. A loyal customer not only continues to buy, but also becomes an advocate for your brand, recommending you to their friends and family. This type of word-of-mouth marketing is extremely valuable and can help your business grow without the need for huge advertising expenditures.

It's also crucial to reinvest in creating new product or service lines. If your business is performing well in one category, it might be time to diversify your offering. Adding complementary products or services can attract new customers and offer more value to existing customers. For example, if you run a clothing business, you might consider adding a line of accessories or shoes. If you offer a consulting service, you could explore creating online courses or downloadable guides. Diversification not only helps you attract more customers, but it can also protect your business from changes in the market. If one product or service line isn't performing well, you'll have other revenue streams to keep your business afloat.

Finally, it's important to maintain a balance between reinvestment and capital accumulation. While reinvesting is essential to scaling your business, you should also make sure you have enough capital available to cover emergencies or take advantage of unexpected opportunities. This means you shouldn't reinvest all of your profits at once. Set a percentage of your income that you will allocate to reinvestment and make sure you keep a reserve fund for unforeseen situations. Financial prudence is key to ensuring your business can continue to grow sustainably without putting its stability at risk.

In short, smart reinvestment is an essential strategy to sustainably scale your business. By identifying key areas that can drive growth, such as marketing, product improvement, team, and technology, and making decisions based on data and planning, you'll be putting your business in a strong position to grow and thrive. Remember that long-term success isn't just about making money, but knowing how to strategically use that money to grow your business and take advantage of new opportunities. By following these principles, you'll see your business not only stay afloat, but grow exponentially over time.

Lucie Dupont

Take Advantage of Online Platforms

Nowadays, if you have a business or are thinking of starting one, taking advantage of online platforms is not just an option, it is a necessity. Digital platforms have revolutionized the way people buy, sell, and connect with each other. In a world where almost everything is just a click away, knowing how to use these tools can make the difference between success and stagnation. Taking advantage of online platforms means using the power of the internet to increase the visibility of your business, attract more customers, and most importantly, increase your sales. In this chapter, I will explain how to do it in a simple and effective way.

The first thing you need to understand is that online platforms allow you to reach a much larger audience than you could ever reach through traditional means. Before, if you wanted to promote your business, you relied on local advertising, newspaper ads, or radio. Now, with the power of the internet, you can get your message out to thousands or even millions of people around the world. Platforms like social media, websites, blogs, and online stores give you the ability to connect with potential customers who otherwise would have no idea you exist. And the best part is that many of these tools are accessible, easy to use, and in some cases, even free.

The first step to taking advantage of online platforms is to have a presence on social media. Social media like Facebook, Instagram, TikTok, LinkedIn, and Twitter are some of the most powerful tools you can use to promote your business. These platforms allow you to not only showcase your products or services, but also interact directly with your customers, receive feedback, and build a closer relationship with your audience. However, it's not just about being on all the networks; it's important to select the platforms that best suit your type of business and your target audience. For example, if you have a fashion business, Instagram or TikTok may be ideal for showcasing your products through images and videos. If, on the other hand, you are dedicated to offering professional services, LinkedIn may be a better option to reach other professionals and companies.

When using social media, it is essential that you create engaging and relevant content for your audience. It is not just about posting photos or promotions of your products, but rather generating content that really interests and captures the attention of your followers. Content can include tutorials, product demonstrations, useful tips, stories behind your brand, or even showing the day-to-day of your business. The more you interact with your audience and the more value you offer them, the more trust you will generate in them, which will translate into more sales in the long run. In addition, social media allows you to run segmented advertising campaigns, meaning you can target your ads specifically to the people who are most likely to be interested in what you offer. This is extremely effective because it maximizes the use of your advertising budget, ensuring that your money is well spent.

Another online platform you should take advantage of is your own website. If you don't have one yet, now is the time to consider creating one. A website is the foundation of your online presence. This is where you can show in detail who you are, what you do, and why customers should choose you over the competition. A well-designed website should be easy to navigate, with clear information about your products or services, and should include a simple way for customers to contact you or make a purchase if you offer online sales. If you sell physical products, consider integrating an online store into your website. Today, there are many platforms like Shopify, WooCommerce, and others that make it very easy to set up an online store, without the need for advanced technical knowledge.

E-commerce is one of the most exciting areas where you can take advantage of online platforms. Whether you sell physical or digital products, having an online store opens the doors to a global market. You are no longer limited to selling only to people in your local area. With an online store, anyone in the world can find and purchase your products. Plus, by having an online store, you can automate many parts of the selling process, meaning you can be making money even while you sleep. Platforms like Amazon, eBay, and Etsy also offer options for selling your products, and they can be a great way to reach customers who are already looking for what you offer.

Aside from having a website or an online store, another platform you can take advantage of is blogging. Blogging allows you to share relevant and useful content for your audience, while at the same time positioning your business as an authority in your industry. A blog can be a powerful tool for driving traffic to your website, as search engines like Google tend to rank websites that offer quality content higher. Writing articles on topics related to your business will not only help you attract more visitors to your website, but it will also increase your customers' trust in you. For example, if you own a pet supply store, you could write about caring for different types of pets, tips for healthy eating, or how to choose the right toy. This type of content shows that you really care about the well-being of pets and are not just trying to sell products.

Another way to take advantage of online platforms is through email. Although sometimes overlooked, email marketing remains one of the most effective ways to stay in touch with your customers. Building an email list allows you to send offers, news, and exclusive content directly to your customers' inboxes. The great thing about email is that you're communicating directly with people who have already shown interest in your business, which increases the chances that they will respond positively to your messages. Tools like MailChimp, Sendinblue, or ConvertKit allow you to create and manage email campaigns very easily. Email is especially useful for building loyalty with your existing customers, as it allows them to stay up to date with your latest promotions or news, keeping them connected to your brand.

In addition to all these platforms, you should not forget about instant messaging apps like WhatsApp and Messenger. These platforms have also become powerful tools for businesses. Through them, you can communicate directly with your customers quickly and efficiently. Many businesses are using WhatsApp Business to send updates, confirm orders, and resolve customer queries in real-time. This kind of more personal communication can help you improve customer experience and increase trust in your brand.

Finally, if you really want to make the most of online platforms, you can't ignore the power of paid ads. While it's possible to attract customers organically – that is, without paying for advertising – the reality is that ads on platforms like Google, Facebook or Instagram can give you a significant boost. Paid ads allow you to reach a wider audience quickly and efficiently, and many platforms allow you to segment your audience in great detail. This means you can show your ads only to people who are most likely to be interested in your product or service, increasing the chances of conversion.

In short, leveraging online platforms is essential to growing your business in the modern world. From social media to email marketing, e-commerce and paid ads, the opportunities are huge. The most important thing is that you use these tools strategically, always thinking about how they can help you attract more customers, improve your visibility and increase your sales. If you do it right, you will see your business start to scale steadily and sustainably over time.

Lucie Dupont

Make Your Business Sell Itself

The dream of any entrepreneur or salesperson is for their business to run almost automatically, for sales to come in constantly without having to constantly chase customers or make manual efforts to close each transaction. Although it may sound like an ambitious goal, with the right strategy, it is possible to create a system where your business practically sells itself. This does not mean that you will not have to work, but that you can establish processes and tools that make sales happen more smoothly and efficiently, without depending so much on your direct intervention. Below I will explain how to achieve this in a practical way.

The first thing you need to make your business sell itself is to have a product or service that actually solves a problem or satisfies a clear need. If what you offer is something that people naturally need or want, it will be much easier to generate sales on an ongoing basis. This is where the value proposition comes into play. You need to make sure that your product or service is sufficiently attractive and differentiating in the market. Ask yourself what makes it special or unique compared to the competition. If you can clearly answer this question and convey that value to customers, you will have taken an important step towards making sales start coming in without much effort. A good product practically sells itself, because when people try it and like it, they will recommend it to others without you having to ask.

Once you have a good product or service, the next step is to create automated systems that help generate sales. This can be achieved through marketing and sales automation. Nowadays, there are many tools that allow you to automate much of the sales process. For example, you can use email marketing software to send automatic emails to your customers every time someone subscribes to your contact list. These emails can include information about your products, testimonials from satisfied customers, special offers, and reminders for customers to buy again. By automating these types of communications, you will be creating a constant flow of interaction with your customers without having to do it manually every time.

Another important tool for automating sales is having a website that is optimized to convert visitors into customers. A well-designed website should be sales-oriented. This means it should be easy to navigate, with a clear and simple purchasing process. If you sell products, make sure customers can buy them directly from your website without any complications. The key here is to reduce friction. The easier it is for your customers to make a purchase, the more likely they are to do so. Additionally, you can integrate tools like chatbots, which can automatically answer frequently asked questions from customers in real time, improving the customer experience without you having to be available all the time.

Social media also plays a big role in this automated sales process. While it may require some initial effort to build a solid presence, once you have an engaged follower base, social media can function as a sales machine that operates almost on its own. You can schedule posts in advance, run automated ad campaigns that showcase your products or services to interested people, and use comments and direct messages to engage with potential customers. Plus, if you create engaging and relevant content, your followers will share it, increasing your visibility without you having to put in any extra effort.

The next key component to making your business sell itself is content marketing. This strategy relies on creating useful, educational, or entertaining content that attracts your target audience and guides them towards purchasing naturally. For example, you can write blogs, create videos, or make social media posts that talk about topics related to your industry or the problems your product or service solves. As more people find your content valuable, they will begin to see you as an authority on the topic, and when they need what you offer, you will be their first choice. Content marketing is an effective way to consistently attract customers without having to always be selling directly.

Another strategy to help your business sell on its own is search engine optimization, better known as SEO. If your website ranks well on Google or other search engines, you will receive organic traffic without having to pay for advertising or make extensive promotional efforts. The goal is that when someone searches for products or services related to what you offer, your website will appear among the first results. To achieve this, you must work on optimizing your site with relevant keywords, creating quality content, and making sure that the user experience on your page is excellent. Although SEO can take time, the long-term results are extremely valuable because the traffic that comes to your page is free and is made up of people who are already interested in what you sell.

In addition to automation and SEO, you should also focus on building long-lasting relationships with your customers. A self-sold business is not just about attracting new customers, but keeping the ones you already have. Customer loyalty is one of the most effective ways to generate automatic sales, as satisfied customers will not only keep buying, but will also recommend you to others. Implementing loyalty programs, offering discounts for repeat purchases, or simply sending thank you emails are all easy ways to keep your customers engaged. The better the experience you offer, the more likely you are to keep customers coming back again and again, without you having to persuade them every time.

Another technique that can help your business sell on its own is word of mouth. When you offer a quality product or service and take care of your customers, they will naturally speak well of you. However, you can incentivize this process by offering referral programs, where current customers receive a benefit every time they recommend your business to others. This can be a discount, a gift, or any other type of incentive that motivates your customers to share their experience with friends and family. By creating these types of programs, you will be making your own customers do the work of promoting you, generating additional sales without any direct effort on your part.

Finally, an important part of making your business sell on its own is establishing strategic partnerships. If you collaborate with other businesses or influencers who have a similar audience to yours, you can leverage their reach to promote your product or service. These partnerships can be very beneficial, as they allow you to reach new customers quickly and effectively. For example, if you own a clothing store, you could partner with an accessories or footwear brand to offer combined products. Or if you offer a consulting service, you could partner with a software provider that complements your services. By joining forces with other businesses, both of you benefit and you can gain additional sales without putting in extra effort.

In short, making your business sell is only possible when you implement a combination of best practices such as automation, content marketing, SEO, customer relations, and strategic alliances. These strategies allow you to build a consistent and efficient sales system, which requires less manual effort and leaves you more time to focus on other areas of growth. Although it won't happen overnight, with patience and the right strategy, you'll see how your business starts to function more autonomously, generating sales almost without realizing it.

Lucie Dupont

From Seller to Investor

Turning from a salesperson to an investor is one of the most exciting and significant steps you can take in your career. When you start selling, your focus is on making money, learning how to close deals, and improving your skills at convincing clients. However, once you master the art of sales and manage to generate consistent income, it is natural to consider how you can make that money grow. This is where the world of investments comes in. Learning to invest wisely will allow you to not only multiply your income, but also build a solid foundation of wealth that will help you achieve financial independence. In this chapter, I will explain how you can make this transition in a practical and effective way.

The first step in transitioning from a salesperson to an investor is to change your mindset about money. As a salesperson, you're probably used to thinking in terms of immediate revenue: how much you make per sale, how many sales you need to make to reach a certain goal, and how you can increase your commissions or income in the short term. This approach is essential in sales, but to become a good investor, you need to think long-term. The key to building wealth through investing is to understand that it's not about making money quickly, but about growing your money steadily and sustainably over time.

Before you start investing, it's important to get your personal finances in order. This means making sure you have an emergency fund - enough money saved to cover your basic expenses in case of unexpected events. An emergency fund gives you the security that you won't have to sell your investments in a hurry if a financial need arises. You should also keep track of your debts. If you have high-interest debts, such as credit cards, it's a good idea to pay them off before you start investing. This is because the interest on those debts can be higher than the returns you could get from your investments. Once your finances are stable and under control, you'll be ready to take the next step.

The next step is to educate yourself about different investment options. In the world of investing, there are many alternatives to growing your money, and not all of them are right for everyone. Some of the most common options include stocks, bonds, mutual funds, real estate, and businesses. Each type of investment has its own risks and benefits, so it's important to do your research and understand how they work before making any decisions. While it can be tempting to let others make decisions for you, it's ideal to actively engage in the process and educate yourself as much as possible. There are many resources available, such as books, online courses, and videos, that can help you learn the basics of how to invest.

If you're new to investing, a good way to start is with simple, accessible investments like index funds. Index funds are one of the easiest and safest ways to invest, especially for beginners. Essentially, these funds are a mix of many different stocks, allowing you to diversify your money without having to buy individual stocks. This reduces risk because instead of relying on the success of a single company, your investment is spread across many companies. Plus, index funds typically have lower fees than other types of investments, meaning more money stays in your pocket.

As you gain experience and confidence, you can explore other forms of investment. For example, if you have an interest in real estate, you might consider investing in real estate. This type of investment can offer you passive income if you decide to buy properties to rent out. Plus, real estate typically appreciates over time, meaning your investment could increase in value over the long term. However, investing in property requires a larger initial capital and a deeper understanding of the real estate market, so it's important to do your research before taking the plunge.

Another interesting option for sellers who want to become investors is investing in businesses. As a seller, you probably understand better than anyone how businesses work and what it takes to make a company successful. This gives you a unique advantage if you decide to invest in startups or emerging companies. You can use your market knowledge and sales skills to identify promising opportunities and help these companies grow. Investing in businesses can be a higher-risk investment, as not all companies succeed, but if you choose well, the rewards can be significant.

Diversification is a fundamental principle for any investor. It means that you should not put all your eggs in one basket. Rather than investing all your money in one asset, such as company shares or property, it is safer to spread your investments across different areas. This reduces risk because if one investment does not perform well, the others can balance out the losses. Think of investments as a table with several legs. If one leg fails, the others keep the table stable. Diversification does not guarantee that you will not lose money, but it can help you reduce the impact of losses and protect your wealth in the long term.

One of the most important lessons you must learn as an investor is patience. Investments, especially those that generate significant wealth, take time to mature. Don't despair if you don't see immediate results. Growing money through investments is a long-term game, and it's often in the later years that you really start to see the impact of your strategy. In fact, one of the most common mistakes among new investors is selling too quickly when the market fluctuates or when an investment doesn't yield immediate results.

Remember that the market has ups and downs, but historically, investments tend to grow over time.

As you build your investment portfolio, it's important to regularly review its performance and make adjustments as necessary. This doesn't mean you should review your investments every day or make constant changes. In fact, many successful investors take a more passive approach, reviewing their portfolio only a few times a year. However, it's important to stay informed about market trends and opportunities that may arise. While you can't predict the future, staying up to date will allow you to make informed decisions and adjust your strategy as needed.

One of the most important benefits of being an investor is that you can generate passive income. Unlike sales, where you typically have to be active and working to make money, investing allows you to make money while you sleep. Dividends from stocks, interest from bonds, and rental income from properties are all examples of passive income you can earn as an investor. Over time, this income can replace your active income, giving you the freedom to work less or even retire early.

Finally, it's important to remember that investing isn't just about making more money, it's about protecting and growing your wealth over the long term. As you advance in your career as a salesperson and investor, you'll develop a greater understanding of how to manage your finances wisely and strategically. The ultimate goal isn't just to grow your money, but to also make sure you're building a solid foundation of financial stability for yourself and your family. When you make the transition from salesperson to investor, you're not only multiplying your income, you're also taking control of your financial future.

In short, the transition from salesperson to investor is a natural step for those who want to grow their money and achieve financial independence. By educating yourself on the different investment options, diversifying your portfolio, being patient, and staying informed, you can become a successful investor and generate passive income in the long term. This path will not only allow you to increase your income, but it will also give you the financial freedom that many seek.